Know Your

Know Your Owls

Jack Byard

Old Pond
PUBLISHING

First published 2016

Published by
Old Pond Publishing,
An imprint of 5M Publishing Ltd,
Benchmark House,
8 Smithy Wood Drive,
Sheffield, S35 1QN, UK
Tel: +44 (0) 114 246 4799
www.oldpond.com

A catalogue record for this book is available from the British Library

ISBN 978-1-910456-26-2

Book layout by Servis Filmsetting Ltd, Stockport, Cheshire
Printed by Replika Press Pvt. Ltd.

Picture credits:
1, 2, 3, 4, 5, 6, 8,11,13, 15,19, 20, 23, 24, 25, 26, 27, 30, 31,32, 33, 34, 35, 36, 38, 39, 40. alan van norman. (7) Antony Grossy (9) Gerardo Marron (10) HYPERLINK "http://www.canopytower.com" www.canopytower.com (12) Dominic Sherony (14) David Evans (16, 18) Greg Lasley (17) Hugh Ranson (21) John van Dort (22) Antonio Guerra (28) Roberto Vargas Masis (29) Neil Morris (37) Chris Sweet.

Also in the 'Know Your' series...

Know Your Bees
32 species of bees, each accompanied by their specific features, including details about their habitat, size and other relevant information

£6.95

Know Your Freshwater Fish
This pocket-sized book provides information about the 54 native, invasive and naturalised species found in the UK today, and includes a photograph of each to allow easy identification

£7.95

Know Your Goats
An illustrated guide to the identification of goats likely to be encountered in Britain today

£4.99

Know Your Sheep
Forty-one breeds of sheep which can be seen on Britain's farms today

£4.99

Know Your Dogs
Forty-five popular dog breeds from Dalmatians to Corgis. Each accompanied with text describing their history, characteristics and abilities

£4.99

Know Your Cats
Covers 42 breeds, each accompanied by a clear description covering the history, appearance and personality of the breed

£4.99

Old Pond PUBLISHING

To order any of these titles please contact us at:
Tel: 0114 240 9930 • Email: contact@oldpond.com • www.oldpond.com
5m Enterprises Ltd., Benchmark House, 8 Smithy Wood Drive, Sheffield, S35 1QN

The eggs are incubated for about a month, and after hatching both male and female hunt to feed the young with caterpillars, beetles, moths and the occasional mouse. It is not known how old they are when they leave the nest but it is believed the parents continue to feed them until they are self-sufficient. Hoot: *bubububububububub.*

Whiskered Screech Owl

Size: 17.5–21cm (6.9–8.3in)
Weight: 85–94g (2.9–3.3oz)
Wingspan: 40–50cm (15.7–19.7in)

The face is a light grey, the eyes are lemon yellow, all surrounded by evenly spaced dark lines. The entire face has a black rim, plus ear tufts and whiskers. The upper body is a brownish grey; the underbody is slightly lighter with dark stripes. The owlets are white

The whiskered screech owl is to be seen in Southern New Mexico, Arizona to Nicaragua, living in dense deciduous forest of oak, walnut, sycamore and juniper, coffee plantations and canyon forests from 1600–2900m (5000–9500ft). Very few nests have been found, but the ones that have been found are in abandoned woodpecker nests and natural cavities in mature trees. The average clutch is three to four eggs and these are laid from April to May.

and northern flicker, up to 10m (35ft) above the forest floor, or in a custom-built nesting box. The average of three to five eggs are incubated for about a month; they then leave the nest before they can fly, and live on the tree branches whilst still being fed by Mum and Dad with beetles, moths, lizards and snakes, for about another five weeks. Hoot: *hoo-hoo-hoo*.

Western Screech Owl

Size: 19–25cm (7.5–10in)
Weight: 131–157g (4.5–5.5oz)
Wingspan: 55–62cm (21.5–24.5in)

The face is a brownish grey surrounded with a fine dark wavy line and spots. The top of the head is brownish grey with buff streaks and wavy lines and short ear tufts. The underbody is a similar colour and pattern. The eyes are bright yellow.

The western screech owl can be heard in western North America, Alaska to western Mexico and east to Texas and Oklahoma. Living in a wide variety of areas but mainly in deciduous and mixed woodland and wooded canyons, they do not like deserts or dense forests as these are the home of the great horned owl, one of its predators. They prefer to nest in cottonwood or large-leaf maple trees in abandoned holes of the pileated woodpecker in large purpose-built nesting boxes. The three to four eggs are laid from late march to mid-April and incubated for about a month; during this time Dad feeds everyone with voles, shrews, rats and mice. After about 45 days they can fly, if not all that well, and are looked after by Mum and Dad for another six weeks. The Ural owl will defend its young aggressively and without fear. Hoot: *wuhu-huwuho-huwuwoo.*

Ural Owl

Size: 50–62cm (19.5–24.5in)
Weight: 630–1020g (22–36oz)
Wingspan: 125cm (49in)

The round face is a dirty off white, framed with tiny white dots, and the eyes are small, dark brown to black. The upper body is a greyish brown with dirty white streaks and spots. The underbody is a similar colour but with large brown streaks

Their territory runs from north Europe to Asia from Scandinavia out to Japan and Korea. They nest in tall trees in open, mature, deciduous mixed forests. The nest is built in natural cavities in tree trunks or hollows that are left where branches have broken off, or in the abandoned nests of large birds and in squirrel dreys. Many of these mature trees with natural nesting places have been chopped down, reducing nesting sites. Many Ural owls now nest two to three eggs and these are incubated for about a month and fledge in about 40 days, but are still dependent on their parents. Hunting takes place mainly in the evening, for mice, rabbits, voles and earthworms, beetles and birds. The young have to find their own territory, and failure means dying of starvation. Red foxes and buzzards are the main predators. Hoot: *ho-hooouh … ho-ho-ho-hoooouh.*

owls, in abandoned woodpecker nests and in tree cavities. The clutch average is three eggs and the incubation and fledging is at the moment thought to be similar to that of other pygmy owls. They hunt during the day and in the evening, feeding on insects, lizards and mice. The species has changed but the hoot is the same: *phew-phew-phew-phew.*

Tawny Owl

Size: 36–40cm (14–16in)
Weight: 325–718g (11.5–25oz)
Wingspan: 99cm (39in)

The head is rounded and the face is a reddish brown with a dark edge and a white 'V' on the forehead. The eyes are bluish black with dark eyebrows. The upper body is a rich tawny colour with lighter mottling and stripes. The underbody is off white to buff. There are more reddish and greyish versions of the tawny owl.

The tawny owl is found in the British Isles, with the exception of northern Scotland and Ireland, and the Iberian coast and across to Asia. Our beautiful tawny friend is at home in old and ancient deciduous woodland and forests and has been seen in the parks of London and Berlin. Breeding takes place from December to mid-March depending on the area. The nests are built in abandoned magpie nests, squirrel dreys and cavities in buildings. The clutch averages

Tamaulipas Pygmy Owl

Size: 13–16cm (5–6.25in)
Weight: 51–57g (1.7–2oz)
Wingspan: 17.78cm (7in)

The male has a brown face with off-white spots; the eyes are yellow with off-white eyebrows. For the male, overall colour is olive brown. The female has similar markings but is a reddish brown.

The Tamaulipas pygmy owl will be seen in the humid evergreen and semi-deciduous forests of Tamaulipas and eastern San Luis Potosi – a small area of north-east Mexico – from 900–1200m (3000–4000ft) above sea level. It is a newly discovered species, originally classified as a pygmy owl, but it has subsequently been found to be an entirely different species, and as such very little is known, but here goes. It builds its nest, as do many runs from August to March depending on the location. The nest is built on the ground or in bushes, always hidden by long grass. The nest holds two to four eggs on average and they are incubated for just over a month whilst the male provides the food. After fledging they remain close to the parents for several weeks. Rats, mice, pigeons and doves are on the menu, but spiny lizards are their favourite. Hoot: *hooOOoh hooOOoh* or *hnnNNNnh*.

Striped Owl

Size: 30–38cm (12–15in)
Weight: 320–556g (11–19.5oz)
Wingspan: 76–81cm (30–32in)

The face is off white with a black surround. The eyes are dark brown with short off-white eyebrows. The ear tufts are long blackish brown with an uncombed look. The underbody is a pale tawny brown with blackish brown streaks. The wings and feathers have light and dark brown bars.

The striped owl can be seen at sunset from southern Mexico to Panama in the northern areas of South America, in Uruguay and northern Argentina, living in semi–open grassland with trees, savannahs and marshland from sea level to 1600m (5000ft). The striped owl does not like to live in dense woodland, and so will never be seen in the Amazon basin. Nesting

food hunt. If the nest is attacked, they will not defend it. After about five weeks, the young will hop onto a nearby branch and it is about ten weeks before their flying is strong enough to hunt for themselves. They hunt for rats, mice, flying squirrels and beetles. Hoot: *whoop-wu-huhoop.*

Spotted Owl

Size: 40.5–48cm (16–19in)
Weight: 520–760g (18.25–27oz)
Wingspan: 107cm (42in)

The face is a pale buff brown with dark concentric circles and a dark rim. The body is dark brown with horizontal white stripes and spots. The breast has off-white and dark bars. The eyes are dark brown, almost black; overall, it is a spotted brown owl.

The spotted owl lives in old mature forests of Douglas fir, redwood, oak and sycamore that are at least 200 years old in North America, British Colombia to Washington and southern California and Texas. This most gentle of owls is now an endangered species. The nests are built in the tops of broken trees and natural tree cavities, and the average clutch is two to three eggs, incubated for about a month, but after two weeks the female will help with the an even larger bird. An average of two eggs are incubated for about five weeks, and the chicks will hop from branch to branch onto a nearby tree before they can fly and will be fed by their parents, still depending on their parents for up to a year after fledging. It is common for only one chick to survive, but they live for about 35 years. Hoot: *pup-pup-pup-pup-po.* The female: *ke-weeeee* like a steam train whistle.

Spectacled Owl

Size: 43–52cm (17–20.5in)
Weight: 590–906g (20.75–32oz)
Wingspan: 76–91cm (30–35.75in)

The eyes are bright yellow surrounded by white – the spectacles. The upper body is dark brown with an off-white or yellow breast. A thin white half collar has a broad brown stripe below.

You will see these owls in Mexico, Central America, down to Argentina and on to the island of Trinidad. They are usually found near water in the dense tropical rainforest with large mature trees, from sea level to 1600m (5000ft). They are mainly nocturnal but will occasionally hunt in the daytime. The spectacled owl can move with great speed once supper is spotted: it will swoop down and snatch anything from a crab to a bat, possum, skunk and a frog and back up to its perch, which is usually hidden in thick foliage to prevent it by being snatched itself for supper by uses abandoned eagles' nests. An average of five to eight eggs are incubated for about a month and the chicks walk from the nest after about 25 days then fledge in about 50–60 days; during this period the male stands guard and feeds the family. Lemmings and voles are their favourite foods plus a wide range of small mammals, ducks and geese. Hoot: *krouff-gouh-gouh-gouk.*

Snowy Owl

Size: 51–68cm (20–26.75in)
Weight: 1134–2000g (40–70.5oz)
Wingspan: 137–164cm (54–64.5in)

Mainly white with dark bars. The eyes are bright yellow with blackish eyebrows. The female has a sprinkling of brown bars and dots, a salt-and-pepper look on the head and the underbody is white with brown dots and bars.

The snowy owl is also called the ghost owl or the Terror of the North, living in many of the arctic regions of Alaska, Canada and Eurasia, and is an occasional winter visitor to the Cairngorms, the Outer Hebrides and the Shetland Isles in the UK. They mainly inhabit the tundra, permanently frozen flatlands without trees. The nests are built on the top of frozen mounds: the female scrapes a hollow with her talons and lines it with her feathers or walking around the nest in about two weeks and flying in about a month. Out of the breeding season, they tend to live in communal groups. Because of high predation by dogs, foxes, ravens and crows, a second brood can be laid. Their food consists mainly of mice and voles, grasshoppers and beetles, hunting occasionally from ground level. Hoot: *voo-hoo-hoo*.

Short-eared Owl

The main body is a mottled brown, and the underbody is a whitish yellow with brownish streaks. The eyes are pale yellow with white eyebrows with a blackish surround. Found in the UK, mainly in the north of England and Scotland out to the Orkneys; also in Scandinavia, Russia and Iceland and across the world to the Hawaiian Islands and North and South America. Living on rough lowland grasses, marshland and sand dunes and occasionally in hedgerows, the short-eared owl will only nest in trees when there is snow on the ground. In marshy areas the nests will be built on small grassy hummocks; on dryer ground in a hollow in the ground, which is then lined with feathers and grass. An average of five to seven eggs are laid at one- to two-day intervals. The young will be

woodpecker nests up to 8m (25ft) high. The RPO lays an average of three eggs and incubates them for about a month and they fledge in about another month but are cared for by Mum and Dad for another three weeks. Their takeaways consist of mice, voles, lizards and the occasional squirrel. In the summer months grasshoppers, beetles and crickets are added to the diet. The main hoot: *whi-whi-whi-whi*.

Ridgway's Pygmy Owl

Size: 17–19cm (6.75–7.5in)
Weight: 46–102g (1.5–3.5oz)
Wingspan: 38cm (15in)

A pale brown face and pale yellow eyes with white eyebrows. Overall, the body is a rusty brown with off-white spots. The chest is off white with rusty-fawn streaks.

The Ridgway's Pygmy Owl can be seen in South Arizona and Texas to Mexico, Sonora and Tamaulipas, south to Panama and north-west Colombia, living in semi-open areas of scrubland with areas of woodland and the occasional giant cactus up to 1500m (5000ft) above sea level. Most of their hunting is done at dusk and dawn and they can be frequently seen roosting on the top of saguaro cactus that can grow up to 45ft high. Breeding takes place in March to June, building their nests in natural tree cavities and abandoned

or cave entrance. The preferred food is rats, snakes, lizards, scorpions and beetles. They have nested on the Egyptian pyramids but holes in trees and hollows in rocky outcrops are more the norm. The two eggs are incubated for about a month, leave the nest in about another month, and continue to be fed and looked after by parents for another six months. Hoot: *buo*.

Pharaoh Eagle Owl

Size: 45–50cm (17.75–19.5in)
Weight: 1900–2300g (67–81oz)
Wingspan: 127cm (50in)

The face is pale fawn with a black rim; the head and upper body are fawn with a mass of black and off-white streaks and blotches. The underbody is off white with black streaks, the chest is rusty brown and lower down the body are rusty-brown wavy streaks (vermiculations). The head has two small ear tufts and the eyes are orange-yellow.

The pharaoh eagle owl can be found from Tunisia to Gambia, Malia, Sudan and from Syria to western Iraq and Oman. It lives in rocky and semi deserts and on dry, rocky mountain slopes with scatterings of shrubs and trees. It roosts during the day and starts hunting when the sun goes down, looking for food from the top of an available tree or a cliff face enabling them to blend in with the local trees. If threatened they will puff out their feathers to look like a tough guy. If that does not work, they will become as slim and tall as possible to look like a tree branch, even swaying in the breeze like the other branches. They live in groups of three or four, called a parliament. Hoot: *grrurr-go-go-go-go*.

Pacific Screech Owl

Size: 23–26cm (9–10.25in)
Weight: 147–170g (5–6oz)
Wingspan: 45.7–61cm (18–24in)

A large round head with prominent ear tufts, the eyes are greyish yellow to yellow. The body is mainly brown with off-white streaks and wavy lines.

Can be found from Oaxaca along the Pacific coast to Costa Rica, living in open landscapes up to approximately 900m (3000ft) above sea level with a scattering of trees and in dry or semi-dry woodland to swampy forests and woods – as long as there are shrubs, the occasional tree and a large cactus they are happy. They nest in abandoned woodpecker nests and lay an average of three to four eggs. Pacific screech owls are true night owls, hunting only at night, feeding on beetles, moths, scorpions and mice. Some are greyer than brown,

mouse. When food is plentiful, they will store it for the bad times. In winter, they will thaw stored food with their body heat. The female is attracted by the singing male – it worked for me. Averages of five to six eggs are laid one to three days apart, incubated for about a month and fledge in another month, although the parents still look after them for another month. Lifespan is about 10 years, 16 in captivity. Hoot: *too-too too too.*

Northern Saw-whet Owl

Size: 17–21cm (6.5–8in)
Weight: 54–120g (1.9–4.2oz)
Wingspan: 45–60cm (17–23.5in)

The upper body is a rusty brown with white spots; the lower body is off white with rusty-brown streaks. The head is large and rusty brown, the face with an off-white area around the bright yellow eyes.

If you are a night owl, you will see our nocturnal friend across North America, southern Alaska and Canada and in the higher landmasses in Mexico. The northern saw–whet lives in coniferous forests and mixed woodland, nesting in abandoned woodpecker holes and even nest boxes anywhere from 2–12m (6–40ft) above the ground. Perching on a branch looking for their next meal, they will silently drop down on their prey: a vole, a harvest mouse or a house

searching for mice, voles, lemmings, also birds and frogs. With their long pointed wings they glide and hover like a 'hawk'. They nest in large cavities in trees and lay between three and 13 eggs. Incubated for about a month, they fledge in another month and leave home in three weeks but stay near Mum and Dad for another two months. Hoot: a bubbling *lulululululu*.

Northern Hawk Owl

Size: 36–41cm (14.17–16.14in)
Weight: 215–392g (7.58–13.83oz)
Wingspan: 78.74–88.90cm (31–35in)

The face is off white with blackish 'cheeks' and the upper body is a greyish brown to dark grey. The top of the head has off-white spots and a white band across the shoulders. The underbody is off white with greyish brown bars. The eyes are golden to pale yellow with white eyebrows.

The northern hawk owl is found in North America from Alaska to Labrador, Eurasia from Norway to Sweden out to Siberia and Northern China and, I am told, occasionally in the UK. Mainly living in open coniferous forests with a mixture of deciduous trees and small clearings, they hunt from exposed lookouts, broken tree stumps and bare branches, old woodpecker nests. This plump little owl feeds mainly on insects, its favourite being grasshoppers, locusts, crickets and beetles. Small mice, birds and mammals are also on the menu. An average of two to four eggs usually hatch at the same time. Mum incubates whilst Dad provides the food. They fledge in about a month but are protected by their parents for another month. Hoot: *gewgaw–gewgaw–gewgew.*

Mountain Pygmy Owl

Size: 15–17cm (5.9–6.69in)
Weight: 52–70g (1.83–2.47oz)
Wingspan: 38cm (14.9in)

The face is pale brown with light and dark speckles. The eyes are yellow with white eyebrows; there are 'false eyes' with off-white surrounds on the back of the head. The upper body is greyish brown with fine white spots. The underbody is off white with an off-white throat and the chest has broad brown vertical stripes.

Found in the highlands of North and Central Mexico from Chihuahua to Oaxaca in the south and north to southern Arizona and New Mexico, mountain pygmy owls live their lives in mountainous pine and evergreen forests and south-facing oak forests above 1500m. Their choice of forest home is also the home of woodpeckers, and the mountain pygmy owl prefers

The weights given are part of the research and unpublished data courtesy of Knut Eisermann, PROEVAL RAXMU Bird Monitoring Program meal. The mottled owl's preferred food is mice, but snakes, frogs and birds are also on the menu. It will also take large insects whilst on the wing. The nests are built in abandoned birds nests or in natural holes in trees where an average of two white eggs are laid between February and May. The young are flying and exploring their surroundings in four to five weeks. Hoot: *gwow-gwow-gwow-gwow-gwot*.

Mottled Owl

Size: 30–38cm (12–15in)
Weight: 176–345g (6.2–12.17oz)
Wing length: 22.1–27.4cm
(8.7–10.75in)

The round head and back are mottled brown, the underbody is off-white with brown vertical bars and streaks on the chest and throat. The eyes are dark brown.

The mottled owl is a native of Central and South America, from Mexico down to Argentina and Brazil, living in variety of woodlands, pine and oak, dry thorn, wet tropical evergreen and on the verges of woodland, from sea level to 2286m (7,500ft). The mottled owl spends its days hidden from the view of predators in thick vegetation and holes in trees. It comes out at dusk where it finds a suitable perch, usually a tree branch, to watch for a possible

ground, they will suddenly pounce. The small prey is swallowed whole and the owls will also take blackbirds and sparrows on the wing. Nesting in well-screened woodland and laying an average of four to five eggs at regular intervals, their young become independent in about three months. Hoot: a low *hoo-hoo-hoo* from 10 to 20 times.

Long-eared Owl

Size: 35–40cm (13.75–15.75in)
Weight: 210–330g (7.5–11.75oz)
Wingspan: 84–95cm (34–36in)

The face is round and off-yellow with a black rim, orange eyes with short off-white eyebrows and prominent ear tufts. The upper body is a mixture of black, brown, grey, buff and white. The underbody is off-white and buff with dark brown streaks and bars.

Also called the pussy owl and the coulee owl, it is found in conifer woods and tree-lined farmland mainly in the north of England and southern Scotland, visiting the more northern parts of Scotland in summer. It is also found throughout Europe, Asia and north-west Africa. The long-eared owl hunts from dusk, and squirrels, bats, moles and shrews are the favourites on the menu. Silently flying and gliding one to two metres above the crevices in walls. The three to six eggs are laid from April to August at two-day intervals, and hatch in about a month. They are able to fly in six to seven weeks and are independent in about three months. They perch on the branch of a tree or a telephone post looking for a tasty takeaway of frogs, beetles and worms. In the 1800s, they were used in households to catch cockroaches. Hoot: *hoo-hoo-hoo.*

Little Owl

Size: 21-23cm (8.27-9.0in)
Weight: 105-260g (3.7-9.17oz)
Wingspan: 56cm (22in)

The head is short and flat. The upper body is a greyish brown with white bars and mottling. The underbody is paler with broad brown streaks, and the eyes are large and yellow with off-white eyebrows.

The little owl is about the size of a starling or a blackbird, and when it was introduced into the UK from Holland in 1899, it was known as the 'fierce little foreigner'. We share our little foreigner with Sweden, Latvia, China and North Africa. It also has a safe haven in Ossett in West Yorkshire. It lives in semi-open landscapes, farmland, stoney deserts and urban areas, and nests in rabbit burrows, holes in trees, preferably old fruit trees, and woodpecker holes, laying three to four eggs. The male hunts whilst the female incubates the eggs. Little is known of their breeding habits but they are known to be fully mature within a year. Hoot: *pupuhp-pupuhp-pupuhp.*

Guatemalan Pygmy Owl

Size: 16–18cm (6.3–7.09in)
Weight: 155–211g (5.5–7.4oz)
Wingspan: 16.4–19.6cm (6.46–7.72in)

The face is a dull reddish fawn with dark stripes from the eyes to the outer edges of the face. The upper body is reddish brown and pale chestnut, and the underbody is off white with reddish brown and with dark vertical streaks. The eyes are yellow.

Found in the mountains of Mexico to Guatemala and Honduras, they hunt mainly at night but can be seen occasionally during the daytime, perched high in the tallest conifer tree in the area looking for their next meal. Rats, mice, insects and other small birds are their favourite food. They are called 'sit and wait' hunters: at the first sight of a meal they will swoop down on their unsuspecting prey. They nest in cavities in dead trees or in old away for later. Nesting can begin in January in old hawk and crows' nests with just a few feathers for comfort. An average of two eggs are incubated for about a month and are able to fly at about two months, but stay close to their parents until the autumn. The great horned owl lives for up to 13 years in the wild and almost 40 in captivity. Hoot: *whoo-whoo-whoo*.

Great Horned Owl

Size: 45–63cm (17.72–25in)
Weight: 900–2503g (31.74–88.29oz)
Wingspan: 91–152cm (35.83–59.8in)

The face is rusty brown to dull yellow with a dark rim, and the eyes are yellow with white eyebrows. Overall appearance a mottled grey brown, the upper body is a brownish fawn, and the underbody is brownish fawn with light and dark bars. The tufts are long and 'uncombed'.

Our great horned friend can be found from just south of the Canadian Arctic down to the pampas plains of South America, inhabiting forest, swamps and deserts on the way. Hunting mostly at night, it looks down from its high perch to swoop on rats, mice and rabbits, or glides slowly and silently just above the ground. If it kills more than it can eat, it will store it and shredded bark. Averages of two to three eggs, laid one to two days apart, are incubated for about a month. Whilst Mum babysits, Dad provides the food, and the chicks fledge in about eight weeks, remaining near home for several months. Great grey owls' favourite food is small rodents; they can hunt by sound alone and will dive into 30cm (12in) of snow to catch a mouse. They live for about 13 years. Hoot: *whooo-ooo-ooo-ooo.*

Great Grey Owl

Size: 61–84cm (24–33in)
Weight: 790–1454g (27.8–51.28oz)
Wingspan: 152cm (59.8in)

A large dark- and light-grey face with dark grey to brownish concentric rings all surrounded by a slim brown border turning white along the bottom edge, with a black beard-like chin. The upper body is greyish brown broken with horizontal mottling, and short dark streaks. The underbody is greyish white with greyish brown streaks. The iris is lemon yellow.

The great grey owl is the largest owl in North America and as such has very few predators. It can be found from California to Alaska, and in Norway, Sweden and Russia. Its home is in conifer forests with open areas and perches from where it forages. The nests are made of sticks, or the abandoned homes of hawks, and are lined with pine needles, deer hair male provides all the food; the young have been seen flying in May. It is sad that so little seems to be recorded about this attractive species. This nocturnal owl roosts during the day away from prying eyes; at dusk it looks down and hunts frogs, lizards and insects. Hoot: *who-wuhu-whhu*.

Fulvous Owl

Size: 40.5–45cm (15.9–17.7in)
Weight: 600–1000g (24.69–35.27oz)
Wingspan: 60–66cm (23.6–25.99in)

The face is pale yellow and darker around the eye; a narrow dark brown rim frames the face. The upper body is a dark reddish brown with off-white and pale buff flecks. The underbody is a fawny reddish brown with brown bars on the neck/shoulder. The eyes are blackish brown with white eyebrows.

The fulvous owl is at home in the highlands of South Mexico, Guatemala, Honduras and El Salvador where it nests in the humid evergreen pine-oak and cloud forests up to 3000m (9840ft) above sea level. The nests are built in natural holes in the tree trunks, providing a home for up to five eggs. The eggs are incubated for about 28 days, and during this time the

nesting site is high, in an abandoned woodpecker nest. The female incubates the two to four eggs for three to four weeks, while her mate provides the food. The young leave the nest after three to four weeks but the parents take care of them for a further four to five weeks. Food is mainly beetles, moths and caterpillars, with the occasional scorpion. They live for about eight years. Hoot: a deep short *hoo* every two to three seconds.

Flammulated Owl

Size: 16–17cm (6.3–6.7in)
Weight: 45–65g (1.59–2.29oz)
Wingspan: 40.64cm (16in)

The face is greyish brown with a semi-transparent reddish brown, washed with pale chestnut. The upper body is a subtle greyish brown with black mottling and stripes, and the shoulders have rusty-orange, buff stripes. The underbody is greyish brown with light and dark rusty spots and black streaks. The eyes are dark brown.

Flammulated owls are found in North America from British Columbia south, running along the Rockies to Mexico, Guatemala and El Salvador. Those living in the northern areas head south in the autumn. The flam gets its name from the flame-like markings on the face. They make their homes in the open coniferous forests with Ponderosa and Douglas pine. Their preferred

They will hunt, from dusk til dawn, anything from a small rodent to young roe deer, including lizards, rats and fish. The two to three eggs are laid in late winter and will not fledge until September to November. They live for 20 years in the wild and up to 60 years in captivity. Hoot: *oohu-oohu-oohu*.

Eurasian Eagle Owl

Size: 58–75cm (23–30in)
Weight: 1550–4200g
(54.67–148.15oz)
Wingspan: 160–188cm (63–74in)

Overall the upper body is blackish brown and fawny showing heavy freckling on the forehead. The underbody is shades of buff with dark streaks; the face is tawny buff with a darker rim and prominent ear tufts. The eyes can be bright red or orange and the tail has six brown bars.

This large, heavy, statuesque owl, with prominent ear tufts and powerful talons, as its name suggests is at home throughout Europe and Asia. There are an estimated 2.5 million within this area, with a small number now breeding in the UK. You will find this owl in coniferous forests, rocky landscapes and quarries and warm deserts; the criterion is the food source.

the ground. In April to May an average of three eggs are laid, incubated for about two weeks and fledge in about a month. They feed mainly on insects and scorpions from which they carefully remove the sting. They live from three to six years in the wild and up to ten years in captivity. Hoot: a high-pitched *whi-whi-whi*.

Elf Owl

Size: 13–14cm (5.12–5.51in)
Weight: 36–48g (1.27–1.69oz)
Wingspan: 27cm (10.63in)

The colour varies between brown and grey. The face is brownish with wavy lines and slim white eyebrows. The upper body is greyish brown with light and dark wavy lines, and the underbody is off white with heavy mottling and wavy lines in greyish brown.

Also known as the Whitney's owl, this tiny owl can be found from south-west USA to Central Mexico. It lives in arid desert where there are plenty of saguaro (a tree-like cactus), thorn scrub or in deciduous woodland near streams, rivers and lakes. The nests are built in old cavities in the saguaro cactus, where they are in competition with the Gila woodpecker who created the cavities in the first place. The nests vary from 3–10m (10–33ft) above eggs will be laid two days apart and fledge after about a month. They hunt in the first four hours of darkness, silently swooping down from their perches on young rabbits, squirrels, small birds and insects. Small prey is swallowed whole, and larger prey is taken back to the nest. Hoot: a mellow mooted trill.

Eastern Screech Owl

Size: 16–25cm (6.3–9.8in)
Weight: 121–244g (4.3–8.6oz)
Wingspan: 46–61cm (18–24in)

The head is large and round, and the face is a pale grey-brown with darker spots or wavy lines. The eyebrows are paler than the rest of the body and the eyes are bright yellow. The ear tufts are short but prominent. The upper body is a greyish black

The Eastern screech owl can be found in most of North America east of the Rocky Mountains, and southern Canada. Its preferred home is in mixed or deciduous woodland with open ground. It will roost in dense foliage, perched on a branch next to the trunk. and nest in cavities in trees, and abandoned nests of the red-bellied woodpecker and northern finch. The nests can be from 1.5–25m (4.9–82ft) above ground level. In April four to eight covering their legs, but the Cuban bare–legged has evolved the cooler feather system for its tropical habitat. It spends its daylight hours hidden away in dense leaf cover or limestone caves, coming to life in the evenings, hunting mainly for insects and occasionally frogs and snakes. Hoot: *coo-coo-coo-gugugug*, getting higher in pitch.

Cuban Bare-legged Owl

Size: 20–23cm (7.75–9in)
Weight: 71–88g (2.5–3.0oz)
Wingspan: 45.75–61cm (18–24in)

The face is a pale buff, and the eyes are brown with white eyebrows. The upper body and the back of the head are dark brown with white spots on the wings; the underbody is pale with white drop-shaped streaks.

The Cuban bare–legged owl is found only in Cuba and the Isla da la Juventud, previously the Isles of Pines, living in forests and woods and limestone caves. The nests are built in, you guessed it, abandoned woodpecker nests and natural tree cavities and crevices in rock faces. It lays an average of two eggs and may use the same nest for many years. Little is known about this owl, and research is ongoing as you read. Most owls have feathers and make the ear tufts more visible. Crested owls build their nest in natural cavities in mature trees and breed between February and September. The female incubates the eggs for about a month and looks after the young whilst the male continues to hunt and provide the food. The young leave the nest in September. Hoot: *k-k-k-k-kkkrrrr.*

Crested Owl

Size: 38–43cm (14.9–16.9in)
Weight: 425–620gm (15–21.9oz)
Wingspan: 56–65cm (22–25.6in)

Mainly chocolate brown including the face, a slightly darker rim around the face disk, and upper chest. The forehead, eyebrows and ear tufts are mostly white. The eyes are dark brown.

Our crested friend nests from south Mexico through Central America, Venezuela to Peru and Bolivia. You will find this forest owl hunting and roosting on the edge of forest clearings and the edge of lowland rainforests up to the magical land where the clouds meet the trees, with a watercourse running through, where it will perch and wait for a passing meal of large insects, caterpillars and beetles. If disturbed it will make itself look slimmer

to Central Oaxaca, the foothills inland of Puerto Angel, from sea level to 1500m (4920ft). The Colima pygmy owl is a small but ferocious hunter, feeding on birds at least twice its size and on mice and insects. The nests are probably abandoned woodpecker holes where it lays between two and four eggs in May. Hoot: *whew-whew-whew* up to 24 times.

Colima Pygmy Owl

Size: 13–15cm (5.11–5.90in)
Weight: 50–65gms (1.52–1.69oz)
Wingspan: 17.78cm (7in)

The face is pale yellow with faint curved lines. The eyes are yellow with short off–white eyebrows. The upper body is a sandy, grayish brown to a greenish brown; the head is round with no ear tufts and has white spots on the crown. The underbody is off white with fawn streaks and brown mottling on the side of the body and three or four visible fawn bars on the tail.

The Colima pygmy owl is another newly recognised species from Mexico. It loves to live in dry tropical woodlands, palm groves, coffee plantations and semideciduous forests, dry oak and thorny woodland on the Pacific slopes from Central Sonora, the foothills of Hermosillo

is known, it is a partial diurnal, daytime hunter, its favourite foods being mice and other small mammals, insects and small birds. It is said to nest in old woodpecker holes and termite nests and lays between two and four eggs. Hoot: *pe—pew-pew-pew*.

Central American Pygmy Owl

Size: 14–16cm (5.5–6.25in)
Weight: 50–57gm (1.76–2.01oz)
Wingspan: 17–18cm (6.75–7.9in)

A round head with no ear tufts, and the face is a pale grey-brown with white speckles. The eyes are yellow with small white eyebrows, the upper body is a rich brown, the underbody off white and the body sides are mottled brown. The tail has four or five off-white broken bands.

The Central American pygmy owl is a newly recognised species found on the lowland Caribbean slopes between Mexico and Costa Rica and in parts of Panama, living in mature but abandoned plantations, but its preferred living and hunting areas are bushland and tropical evergreen forests up to 1300m (4200ft) above sea level. An owl about which little

hours, feeding on mice and other small mammals, insects, spiders and grasshoppers in the winter months, some of which it stores. They lay an average of three to seven eggs that take about a month to incubate, and during this time the male will bring food and defend the nest against predators. Hoot: *hoo hoo*, sometimes preceded by a *huhuhu*.

Cape Pygmy Owl

Size: 15–16cm (6–7in)
Weight: 50–65gms (1.8–2.3oz)
Wingspan: 368–406mm (14.5–16in)

The upper body is a sandy, grayish brown with a reddish tinge; the underbody is off white with fawny, brown streaks. The head is brown without ear tufts and the eyes are yellow with white eyebrows.

The cape pygmy owl is found in California in the Sierra de la Laguna mountains, living in the pine and oak woodlands at altitudes of 1500–2000m (5000–6500ft). In the winter it sensibly moves to a slightly warmer altitude of about 500m (1640ft). Little is known, or written, about the nesting habits, but it is known to nest in natural tree cavities and old woodpecker holes. The cape pygmy owl is diurnal, meaning it is active during daylight snack delivered to the door. They lay up to 12 eggs, a day apart, hatching within two weeks and flying the nest within seven weeks. The young will make a noise like a rattlesnake to scare away predators. They live for about seven years; their main enemies are hawk owls and falcons. Hoot: a two-note *coo-coooo*.

Burrowing Owl

Size: 19–28cm (7.5–11.0in)
Weight: 140–240gms (4.9–8.5oz)
Wingspan: 50.8–61cm (20–24in)

The upper part of the body and the round head are brown, the bright eyes have white eyebrows, and the chin/throat is white. The underbody is white with brown spots or bars. The wings have light and dark bars, and a brown tail has three paler bars.

The burrowing owl inhabits the Americas, living in open grassland and land with minimum vegetation, including deserts. They live in the abandoned burrows of prairie dogs, skunks and armadillos and are sometimes called the prairie dog owl. Hunting from dawn until dusk, they catch insects and beetles during the day and small mammals and reptiles after dusk. They surround their burrow with animal waste to attract dung beetles: their favourite to the size of a pigeon, and the occasional fish. If disturbed it will camouflage itself against a tree trunk or silently fly deeper into the forest. Brown wood owls build nests in tree cavities or in the forked trunk of a tree and line the nest with feathers. The average clutch is two eggs that are incubated for about a month. It lives for about 15 years in captivity, but because of its secretive nature, information on the brown wood owl is limited. Hoot: *who-whoowwwwooh*.

Brown
Wood Owl

Size: 34–45cm (13.75–17.7in)
Weight: 800–1100g (28.2–38.8oz)
Wingspan: 94–130cm (77–51in)

The face is rusty brown with a faint black surround. The brown eyes are surrounded by a blackish area and the blackish brown head has a rusty tint. The collar is a tawny-buff. The main body is a light chestnut with dark brown bars; the underbody has fawn and brown streaks.

Found in southern India, Burma, Thailand, Borneo and West Java and in various sanctuaries throughout the British Isles, this secretive owl spends its life in heavy deciduous and evergreen tropical forests. During the day, it perches in tall trees having a snooze and comes to life in the evening, hunting for a meal of rats and mice, fruit bats and insects and birds up

and beetles. Up to
eight eggs can be laid
at one-day intervals.
They fledge in about a
month but the parent
will look after them for
up to six weeks. They
are hunted by other
larger owls and birds
and the pine marten.
Hoot: *po-po-po-po*.

Boreal Owl

Size: 20–30cm (8–12in)
Weight: 102–157g (3.5–5.5oz)
Wingspan: 55–62cm (22–25in)

The face is white with a dark rim and small white spots. The upper body is dark brown with strong white spots. The underbody is off white with broad dark streaks, close together on the chest and less so lower down. The brown tail has four or five horizontal white bars. The eyes are yellow.

A small owl found across Europe, where it is also known as the Tengmalm, and North America. It is found in many locations but mainly in older, dense deciduous and coniferous forests where holes, 5–6m (16–20ft) up, left by woodpeckers, make ideal nesting spots. Boreal owls feed on mice, voles and shrews but are not averse to snacking on frogs, bats

the forest floor. It nests in holes in rotting tree stumps and will breed from March to May depending on the availability of food. It normally lays two eggs and the young fly the nest in about two months. They live for about 20 years in the wild and 29 years in captivity. Hoot: *wobobobobobo-wow-ho.*

Black and White Owl

Size: 30–40cm (12–16in)
Weight: 404–535g (14.25–19oz)
Wing length: 272mm (11in)

The face is mainly black with white speckled eyebrows over dark brown eyes. The neck and underbody is covered with black and white stripes. The upper body is covered with white stripes.

Black and whites are generally solitary birds but can be seen in small groups in rainforest clearings and flooded woodland with semideciduous mixed with evergreens. Their dark faces and stripes make them almost invisible in the dark. Their evening meal consists of insects, small mice, rats and even bats, which they occasionally catch whilst in silent flight. Watching from a hidden perch, the black and white swoops down and scoops its prey off

is usually two to four eggs, hatching in four weeks and fledging in about five weeks. In the wild they live for about 10 years and 23 years in captivity. Hoot: sounds like *'Who cooks for you, who cooks for you all.'*

Barred Owl

Size: 40–43cm (16–25in)
Weight: 500–1050g (17.6–36.96oz)
Wingspan: 96–125cm (38–49in)

A large solid-looking owl with a round head, a pale face and brown eyes surrounded by dark rings. The upper body is mottled grey brown with horizontal bars, the underbody is lighter with vertical streaks. The tail has three to five white bars.

A common sight in North America from California and now seen as far north as Canada living in deciduous and pine-type forests, perched high in the treetops looking for a possible meal, mainly mice, shrews and rabbits. The opportunity of a meal is not to be missed, and barred owls can fly off with a fully grown family cat. They will occasionally hunt before dark during the breeding season – January in the south and April further north. The clutch

They return to the same site year after year. The average is three to six eggs, which will fledge in around 50 days. Their food consists of voles, shrews, young rats and mice, swallowing them whole. This is not a hooting owl, but has an ear-piercing shriek.

Barn Owl

Size: 33–39cm (13–15in)
Weight: 250–480g (8.8–16.9oz)
Wingspan: 80–95cm (31–37in)

The face is heart shaped. The discs around the eyes are white with a brown edge. Overall, the upper body is shades of brown with black and white speckles. The underbody is mainly white with tear-shaped spots, the wings are banded brown.

The barn owl can be found throughout the British Isles and every continent with the exception of Antarctica. It can usually be seen in open heath, moorland and woodland, and the nests are built in old buildings including church spires and even the Yankee Stadium. As the feathers are not waterproof, a watertight home is essential. Barn owls mate for life and can breed at any time during the year depending on the quantity of food available.

balsas, but it is believed it feeds on small mouse-like creatures and insects. I am told that no one has yet described the nest but the assumption is that it lives in tree cavities and breeds in June. Hoot is like a bouncing ball: *hooh-hooh-huh-nuh-huhuhurrr*. Yes!

Balsas Screech Owl

Size: 27cm (10.5in)
Weight: 150–174g (5.29–6.17oz)
Wing length: 170–185mm (6.7–7.3in)

Mainly grayish brown with large brown eyes with a dark brown surround with paler rims. The upper body has dark brown streaks and dark wavy lines. The underbody is paler with dark wavy streaks and short ear tufts.

The balsas is the largest of the screech owls and is found only in a small area in central western Mexico, living and hunting at altitudes of 600–1500m (1900–4900ft). Its hunting grounds are dry thorn forests. The thorny trees are scattered and average about 7–8m (23–26ft) tall. It perches on tree stumps and in the trees, where it is difficult to spot as its plumage provides superb camouflage against the bark of the trees. Little is known about the about its breeding habits, but it nests in natural cavities in trees, rocky crevices and abandoned buildings. It is also accepted that the period from the three to seven eggs being laid to fledging is similar to the barn owl, about 50 days. Hoot: rapid clicks followed by a two- to three-second raspy wheeze. I know the feeling well.

Ashy-
Faced Owl

Size: 26–43cm (10–17in)
Weight: 200–400g (7.1–14.1oz)
Wingspan: 106cm–119cm (42–47in)

The heart-shaped face is ash grey with an orange-brown surround; the upper body is yellow-brown with black wavy lines. The under body is yellowish brown with dark arrow-shaped spots. The eyes are black-brown.

The ashy faced owl was originally believed to be a sub species of the barn owl but it is now accepted as being an entirely different species. It is found only in the Dominican Republic and Haiti, living in lowland forest and forest edges where trees with large enough cavities can be found. As the forest shrinks and disappears, so do the nesting cavities and the ashy faced owl. Its diet consists of mice, rats, tree frogs, snakes and insects. Little is written

Credits

I have so many people to thank for their help and advice in the writing of this book, among them alan van norman, for his generosity in supplying most of the photographs, and Knut Eisermann, who despite their extremely busy lives, found time to answer my never-ending list of queries, and to Tony of Maple Leaf Images Skipton for his help and advice. Not forgetting my wife Elaine for an incessant supply of full stops and commas. Thanks also to my friends, young and mature, who, so they tell me, still enjoy the books. Long may it continue, please.

Foreword

The beautiful owl has been around for almost 6 million years and there are fossils and cave paintings to prove it. Modern man has been around for a mere 200,000 years. Owls have for many thousands of years been loved, feared and hated in equal measure. It is still the same in these modern and enlightened times: they are the bringers of good health and fortune, or a sign of bad luck and worse. Little has changed.

There are over 200 species of owl that have served us in many ways, from keeping grain stores free of insects, rats, mice and other unwanted vermin, a task they still excel at in vineyards and orchards. A nest of two adults and four young will eat up to 1000 mice, voles, etc. during the nesting season, the young alone eating four each a day.

The owl cannot move its eyes, but to make up for this it can turn its head 270°. It also has three eyelids: the outer eyelids are normal, the upper lid closing when blinking, the lower lid closing for sleeping, and the third is a very fine membrane that moves diagonally across the eye to clean and protect the surface of the eye. The owl's fantastic long sight, exquisite hearing, silent flight and patience are the main tools in its hunting arsenal.

Owls, for the average person, do not make good pets unless you have the skills to take good care of a wild creature; to take on an owl without the necessary skills is extreme cruelty. You are not Harry Potter. Please enjoy the beauty of owls in their natural surroundings or in owl sanctuaries specialising in the rehabilitation of sick and injured owls and the conservation of these beautiful creatures.

Contents